PHAEDRA

A.T.L.

AMERICAN THEATER IN LITERATURE

PHAEDRA

Matthew Maguire

LOS ANGELES
A CREATION PRODUCTION COMPANY /
HOME FOR CONTEMPORARY THEATRE
AND ART BOOK
SUN & MOON PRESS
1995

Sun & Moon Press
A Program of The Contemporary Arts Educational Project, Inc.
a nonprofit corporation
6026 Wilshire Boulevard, Los Angeles, California 90036

This book was first published in paperback in 1995 by Sun & Moon Press
10 9 8 7 6 5 4 3 2 1
FIRST EDITION

This book was made possible, in part, through an operational grant from the Andrew W. Mellon Foundation and through contributions to The Contemporary Arts Educational Project, Inc., a nonprofit corporation

Cover and Design: Drenttel Doyle Partners, New York
Typography: Guy Bennett

LIBRARY OF CONGRESS CATALOGING IN PUBLICATION DATA
Maguire, Matthew
Phaedra
p. cm—(American Theater in Literature Program)
ISBN: 1-55713-242-9
1. Title. II. Series.
811'.54—dc20

Printed in the United States of America on acid-free paper.

Phaedra was first presented at Here Theatre in New York on April 7, 1995. It was co-produced by HOME for Contemporary Theatre and Art (Randy Rollison, Artistic Director; Barbara Busachino, Producing Director) and Creation Production Company (co-Artistic Directors, Matthew Maguire and Susan Mosakowski), with the following cast:

FAYE	Socorro Santiago
THOMAS	George Bartenieff
WILLIAM	Andy Paris
ANGUS	Ray Xifo
NONNY	Verna Hampton
ARICIA	Nicole Alifante

Director: Matthew Maguire; Set Design: Elizabeth Diller and Ricardo Scofidio; Light Design: Roma Flowers; Costume Design: Suzanne Gallo; Choreography: Patricia Hoffbauer; Stage Manager: Lisa DeRensis.

Characters:

FAYE	
THOMAS	Faye's husband, a CEO
WILLIAM	Thomas' son
ANGUS	tutor and friend to William
NONNY	once Faye's nanny; a life-long friend
ARICIA	daughter of the chairman of a multinational corporation ruined by Thomas in a hostile takeover

Setting:

The present moment. An upper class American home. Night.

Act One

FAYE *wanders in the night murmuring expressions of lust as she tries to find her way out of an invisible maze.*

FAYE: Take me...

Light strikes a chair. FAYE *approaches it. She sits. She struggles to understand what is happening to her.* THOMAS *enters. He touches her. She doesn't respond.*

THOMAS: Couldn't sleep.

FAYE: Neither can I.

THOMAS: Why not?

FAYE: I don't know.

THOMAS: What are you doing?

FAYE: Thinking.

THOMAS: About what?

FAYE: Nothing.

THOMAS: Some tea?

FAYE: No.

•

WILLIAM *is relaxing with his head in* ANGUS' *lap.*

ANGUS: Why do you sleep alone?

WILLIAM: So I can breathe.

ANGUS: Don't you ever feel the urge…to…[*at a loss for the word*]

WILLIAM *wryly completes* ANGUS' *thought with a lewd gesture.*

Well…yes—all right. Don't you?

WILLIAM: Of course.

ANGUS: Then?

WILLIAM: Then *what*?

ANGUS: If you don't marry and have a child, what happens to the family line?

WILLIAM: That's a funny thing to ask a bastard.

ANGUS: Fine. Mock your father. I'll be the first to join you. He's made it his life's mission to fertilize the Western world. But you're his son in every way—it's time you faced it.

WILLIAM: I don't want to stick my head into a domestic trap of squalling infants. I want the wildness of taming horses.

ANGUS: If you don't breed, the air will be a place where nothing moves.

WILLIAM: I love that place. I long for that place.

ANGUS: You're shaking.

WILLIAM: I didn't sleep at all last night. I worked in the stables till one and went straight to bed. I was flooded by a dream of such erotic power I felt I was possessed.

ANGUS: You, the man who's turned his back on love?!

WILLIAM: I awoke in a fever certain the embarrassment of some nocturnal emission would await me. And yes, there it was, but it glistened like quicksilver. I scraped this substance off the sheet and took it to a lab. It was mercury. The growing chaos of my life is so frightening I'm hard pressed not to run to a priest.

ANGUS: Who's the woman?

WILLIAM: I can't say.

ANGUS: Oh come on.

WILLIAM: No.

ANGUS: Why don't you give in? You're in love, it happens to everyone. All right—you said it'd never happen to you. Do you think anyone took you seriously?

WILLIAM: [*smelling the air*] She must've been here.

ANGUS: Who?

WILLIAM: I have to leave this place.

ANGUS: [*stroking* WILLIAM'S *head*] Not yet.

WILLIAM: The walls are too thin and they sweat unknown liquids. The angles are unnatural.

ANGUS: If you leave, your father cuts you off. You'll never get your horse farm.

WILLIAM: The air smells like rutting bodies.

ANGUS *rubs* WILLIAM'S *chest.*

WILLIAM: No.

ANGUS *doesn't stop.* WILLIAM *pushes his hands away.*

Stop.

They make their way into the sitting room where the household is gathered, mid-conversation, after dinner. When WILLIAM *sees* ARICIA *he instinctively turns to go, but* ANGUS *restrains him.*

NONNY: I'm so sorry they found little Anastasia's bones.

WILLIAM: All royalty should be found in shallow graves.

FAYE *notices* WILLIAM *and suddenly hears and sees no one else.*

THOMAS: Watch your tongue. You forget who we are?

WILLIAM: I can't.

THOMAS: Bigger than the Romanovs ever were.

FAYE: They had a certain permission.

THOMAS: And obligations.

FAYE: Have you ever thought about that?

WILLIAM *is drawn towards* ARICIA.

WILLIAM: That I've inherited some deadly noblesse oblige?

FAYE: No.

THOMAS: You've inherited nothing yet!

ARICIA: [*directly in* WILLIAM'S *face*] Is that so?

FAYE *takes* WILLIAM'S *arm and leads him away.*

FAYE: Have you?

WILLIAM: What?

FAYE: Thought.

WILLIAM: Of what?

FAYE: Permission.

NONNY: Well, we don't need one.

ANGUS: What?

NONNY: A samovar.

THOMAS: That's right, damn Ruski bullshit, they didn't waste any time building a mafia.

FAYE: Have you ever thought about it?

ANGUS: [*to* THOMAS] It was bound to happen.

THOMAS: I don't believe anything is *bound* to happen.

ANGUS: A pure market is an oxymoron.

THOMAS: How're we supposed to prop them up when they've sold their whole damn system to the black market?

FAYE: Permission.

ARICIA: [*referring to* ANGUS] He's right, it's inevitable.

WILLIAM: I don't think I understand what you're saying.

NONNY: Would anyone like a cognac or a sherry?

FAYE: [*taking* WILLIAM'S *hand*] I think you do.

NONNY: Faye? [*she doesn't answer*] Faye?

ARICIA: I could go for something, sure.

NONNY: Thomas?

THOMAS: They're using their rubles for wallpaper.

NONNY: Thomas, are you listening?

ARICIA: Always.

WILLIAM: [*subtly trying to remove his hand*] No.

ANGUS: [*to* WILLIAM] Come on, do you good.

THOMAS: Yes, I'll take a Hennesey. William?

Everyone looks at WILLIAM *trying to extricate himself from* FAYE*—their hands glow with their own light.* FAYE *lets go.*

THOMAS: [*leaving*] I'm going out.

ARICIA: [*relishing the barb*] We won't wait up.

ARICIA *and* ANGUS *manage an awkward exit.* WILLIAM *and* FAYE *stare at one another as he backs out the door. She sits in the chair which affects her like a vehicle for erotic transport. Catching herself, she leaps from the chair and stares at it as if it's possessed. She runs out, leaving a startled* NONNY *alone.* NONNY *tries to deny her rising despair over* FAYE'S *destructive turn.*

NONNY: All quiet now.

She notices a tea bag on the side of a saucer and lifts it.

A flea bag! What a delight!

She sees a corset lying on a chair.

Look at this! An old-fashioned corset! Now who's been sinkin' their teeth in this?

The hooks and eyes unravelling, eyes still hungry for hooks, hooks still yearning to jump through eyes. Like the hoops of a flea circus. The fleas leap from their bags, through the eyes, and straight onto the hooks. Meat hooks for the miniature, skewers for the carcasses of insects. Dead professionals. No longer ready to do their heady tricks.

But if they were alive they could perform on my body. Lilliputians, clamboring over the nooks and hooks and crooks and crannies of my fanny's one-ring circus. Ahh, the big top swarming with little tops. They scurry across the ring and pop through the eye and down the drain into the veins of my love.

My love, my love... [*moaning*] Ohhhhhh... Where is he? Mouldering in the grave, my poor old lover. Bone man in the bone yard.

ANGUS *walks in with an armful of cabbage.*

NONNY: You frightened me.

ANGUS: Me?

NONNY: Your body looked as if it was painted on by a gothic devil.

ANGUS: You drinking again?

NONNY: Your crotch was a bloated tulip with petals painted like membranes.

ANGUS: I'm a gardener, not some demon.

NONNY: No, you're the tutor.

ANGUS: Was.

NONNY: Are.

ANGUS: As you will.

NONNY: You hear them again last night?

ANGUS: They're just babies.

NONNY: But Faye acts like she's dying. She can't soothe them. You don't know what I'm going through. I can't help her.

ANGUS: What's wrong with her?

Pause. NONNY *evades the question.*

NONNY: I wish we could soundproof the nursery.

ANGUS: [*grunting*] Hmm.

NONNY: Does that sound callous?

ANGUS: Not as bad as baking them for dinner.

NONNY: They suckle so hard they've worn out three wet nurses.

ANGUS: Hungry little buggers.

NONNY: And Philly's gettin' teeth, so I know the new one's gonna quit any day.

ANGUS *puts away the cabbage.* NONNY *sneaks a drink.* ARICIA *walks in and catches her.*

ARICIA: Nothing like a good stiff shot on the sly.

NONNY: Listen here, you little Miss-whatever-you-are, I ought to scratch—

She is interrupted by FAYE *entering.*

FAYE: Nonny, draw me a bath, please.

NONNY: You've already had three.

FAYE: [*leaving*] One more.

NONNY: [*glaring at* ARICIA, *as she leaves*] You'll have to excuse me.

Pause.

ANGUS: You've upset this house.

ARICIA: It didn't start with me.

ANGUS: Why don't you leave William alone?

ARICIA: You know why.

ANGUS: His father will never accept you.

ARICIA: If I could work or live anywhere else I would, but Thomas blocks my every move. When he *invited* me to live here, what he really meant was "welcome to your cell."

ANGUS: If he catches you with his son, you'll never get out.

ARICIA: What excites me the most is the challenge. Imagine the thrill of seducing someone who swears he'll never love.

ANGUS: Won't work. Your ambition's too obvious.

ARICIA: You're wrong about me. It's beyond ambition. Watching him struggle against what he wants so much—that arouses me.

ANGUS: The chance to regain your position is more like it.

ARICIA: The boy doesn't know he's in love with lust, and he's found an infinite delay mechanism. Cranks me like a bitch in heat.

WILLIAM *enters. He stops short when he sees* ARICIA. NONNY, *right behind him, pulls him aside.*

NONNY: William, I need to tell you something. [*pause*] Faye's dying. I don't know of what.

WILLIAM: I know.

•

Alone, FAYE *dances in awkward lurches because her yearning won't let her be still. She hears* THOMAS *coming and stops. He sits and opens the market listings.* FAYE *embraces him from behind. As he responds she moves away, silent. He waits.*

FAYE: Make him go.

THOMAS: He's my son.

FAYE: And I'm your wife. [*pause*] Aren't I?

THOMAS: It'd make me look weak.

FAYE: Can't you find a way?

THOMAS: The market could crash on the rumors alone.

FAYE: Can't you separate this from business?

THOMAS: I want him to take over the firm when I retire.

FAYE: What about *our* sons?

THOMAS: They're still nursing, for chrissakes!

FAYE: What does that matter?

THOMAS: Will's first in line.

FAYE: He's the bastard child of your fling with some Amazon!

THOMAS: You promised you wouldn't!

FAYE: Our sons deserve better. And he knows what's at stake, that's why he hates me.

THOMAS: That's simply not true.

FAYE: You have to trust me.

THOMAS: [*pause*] I do.

FAYE: Then send him away before it becomes a crisis.

THOMAS: What has he done to offend you?

FAYE: The way he looks at me.

THOMAS: It's only natural a young man might have some resentment for a stepmother. Don't take it personally.

FAYE: Have you seen how he looks at me?

THOMAS: I haven't seen him look at you at all.

She is silent, moves away.

What if it came out that the only reason is "my wife wanted it?"

FAYE: Thomas, [*pause*] I hate him.

THOMAS *walks out. Alone,* FAYE *is driven back to her awkward dance.*

FAYE: William...William...oh Will...

Bodies lying in a heap, grunting, rutting. It's so laughable; the grotesque shapes the flesh can make. Organs jutting out like red nosed clowns, or hiding coyly, or parading HMS Pinafore engorged. Spewing drops of fluid like fluttering pigeons, those awkward birds that waddle so crudely, yet, when swooping together in their relentless circles so hypnotically beautiful. Thrusting. Will he love me? So silly, makes me want to weep. I have no body. Nothing but a swirling mass of contradictions. All so balled up that it looks like flesh, but it's really petrified struggles. My lips the hardening of a million cries. My breasts the calcification of countless howlings. Can he love me? Yes, yes, yes. My skin will soothe him. Luscious juices like marraca rinds pouring in his ears, whispering, always whispering, "Love me." Even though my body is a mirage, love me.

Murmuring "love me" over and over, FAYE *implodes.*

NONNY *enters and finds* FAYE *out of control.*

NONNY: Darling, what's wrong?

FAYE: I need more light.

Their cries pile on top of one another.

NONNY: Why don't—[you turn on the lamp?]

FAYE: Light to wash away—

NONNY: What are you—[talking about?]

FAYE: Wash away this... [*she can't say*]

NONNY: Faye, what's—[wrong with you?]

FAYE: More light, more light, more light!

NONNY: [*turning on a lamp*] That's easy.

FAYE: No! Turn it off, turn it off!

NONNY: But you said—[you wanted more light]

FAYE: I've never had light, always shadows, bring me shadows, more shadows!

NONNY *seizes* FAYE *to calm her. They struggle.*

NONNY: Calm your—[self!]

FAYE: Shadows—

NONNY: Stop this—[craziness!]

FAYE: I need the dark—

NONNY: Please!

FAYE: Shadows, shadows…

FAYE *collapses in* NONNY'S *arms.*

NONNY: There, there…there, there…there, there…

FAYE: I belong in the dark.

NONNY: What's the matter with you, my little one?

FAYE: Nonny dear, please don't call me that.

NONNY *tightens her vise-like grip on* FAYE.

NONNY: My little one.

FAYE: Don't call me that.

NONNY: My little one.

FAYE: Don't call me that.

NONNY *turns away, hurt.*

FAYE: Come here.

FAYE *hugs her.*

It's worse than when my mother…it's worse.

NONNY: What's wrong?

FAYE: There's nothing but constant slashes.

NONNY: What is it?

FAYE: I can't see it.

NONNY: Try.

FAYE: I can't.

NONNY: Why won't you tell me?

FAYE: I can't.

NONNY: You mean you won't.

FAYE: I said I can't.

NONNY: Who raised you?

FAYE: Please.

NONNY: I know when you're holding something back. If you think you can shut me out, I think it's time I left this house.

FAYE: [*grabbing her arm*] Nonny—

NONNY: How can I watch you starve yourself to death and never ask why?

FAYE: I can't.

NONNY: How many pounds this month! I'll have to hospitalize you, and I'm not supposed to—[know why?]

FAYE: No!

NONNY: Then who am I?

FAYE: I love you.

NONNY: Then let me help you.

FAYE: I don't know how.

NONNY: If you're lost, I'm lost.

FAYE: I know.

NONNY: I'm afraid you're going to die.

FAYE: I am.

NONNY: No!

FAYE: It's the only way.

NONNY: I'm not going to watch you die.

FAYE: What are you doing?

NONNY: Leaving.

FAYE: No.

NONNY: Well?

Pause. FAYE *can't speak.* NONNY *turns to go.*

FAYE: Don't leave me.

NONNY: Tell me, or I walk out now.

FAYE: All right.

FAYE *hesitates.* NONNY *waits.*

I keep dreaming of a bull, a sweating black bull, its flanks are heaving and its enormous rod is full and pulsing. He snorts and phlegm shoots out his nostrils, they're gaping pink and chafed. He stamps his right hoof in the dust and an Arabian carpet appears. He lowers his engorged loins onto the carpet and pumps his thick tool over the intricate design. A bull's cock plunging through the labyrinth. It's William.

NONNY: God help you.

FAYE: Too late.

NONNY: You mustn't tell Thomas.

FAYE: And you mustn't.

NONNY: I'd pull all my teeth first.

FAYE: Now will you let me die in silence?

•

WILLIAM: [*whispers*] Aricia, where are you?

ARICIA: I'm in the Pure Room. Bathing in come. In.

WILLIAM: I can't.

ARICIA: Come in.

WILLIAM: I can't.

ARICIA: Come soon.

WILLIAM: Whisper.

ARICIA: Whisper to me.

WILLIAM: Soon.

ARICIA: I don't dare look at the walls.

WILLIAM: Close your eyes.

ARICIA: Come to me.

WILLIAM: I can't.

ARICIA *charges at* WILLIAM, *their bodies strike like animals in combat. They fall, tangled.*

ARICIA: Kiss me.

WILLIAM: I'm too afraid.

ARICIA: What can you do?

Pause.

WILLIAM: Tell you a story?

ARICIA: Yes.

WILLIAM: It's about distance.

ARICIA: Distanza.

WILLIAM: The ship was sailing.

ARICIA: La nave salpava.

WILLIAM: The waves licking at its hull.

ARICIA: The bow splitting the foam.

WILLIAM: Water, luscious water.

ARICIA: The ship yearning to rise above the waves.

WILLIAM: The waves clutching with hungry fingers. The ship tumbling, sliding down viscous ridges of distance.

ARICIA: How many days, how many years? have we been…

WILLIAM: Have we been at…

Long pause.

ARICIA: Sea.

WILLIAM: Are your hands chafed?

ARICIA: Is your skin raw?

WILLIAM: It's been so long.

•

FAYE *walks to the chair, stares at it, sits and crosses her legs. The light grows brighter on her face.*

ANGUS: Faye plays with the top button of her blouse.

NONNY: You keep your lizard's tongue off the mistress.

ANGUS: Her eyes radiate. Her thighs part. Is she thinking of a lover?

NONNY: She's thinking of her husband.

ANGUS: You know she's not.

NONNY: When did a tutor get the second sight?

ANGUS: From my wife. My love had a growth in the small of her back, a sac of tranquillity, an elegant membrane. The sac was bulbous, traced with a lacework of faint blue veins. It sang. Nothing vulgar, no caterwauling in the shower. No. This was a sound that if I lay my head near it, say—on her shoulders—I could hear it faintly, as if it were coming from some great distance. It made many kinds of music depending on her mood. Sometimes Puccini, sometimes a tango. [*He sings a melody*] The surgeon wanted to remove it. She refused. You'd never know it caused her any problem. Ain't no other suffered like my lover. Things grow. Grass grows through concrete. The essence of life is miraculous.

NONNY: You're gettin' above yourself.

ANGUS: After she died I kept that sac. Helps me see things.

NONNY: Liar.

ARICIA *and* WILLIAM *enter from opposite sides of the room.*

ANGUS: Madam's thinking of the chair in the sunlight. And, yes, of course she's thinking of a lover. But the lover is not hers.

ARICIA: Did you say something?

ANGUS: Faye is thinking of a room in which sits William. William is thinking.

WILLIAM: Did you say something?

ANGUS: William is thinking of another room in which sits Aricia.

FAYE: There's going to be a flood.

NONNY: [*knowing too much*] Faye, don't.

ANGUS: Madam, it hasn't rained in years.

FAYE: It'll fill this room. I've seen it.

ANGUS: What do you mean? we're on high ground.

FAYE: I can see it.

FAYE *shows them the marks of high water lines on the walls.*

FAYE: Look at this, eleven years ago, and here, seventeen.

Disturbed, NONNY *and* ANGUS *exit swiftly.* FAYE, *with a reluctant glance at* WILLIAM, *follows.*

•

WILLIAM: Why do you stay?

ARICIA: Why do you?

WILLIAM: There's something I have to do.

ARICIA: I feel the same.

WILLIAM: But he destroyed your family.

ARICIA: No. My father's arrogance did that. He left the company vulnerable by expanding too fast and acquiring too much debt. He swore no one would ever dare a takeover.

WILLIAM: But my father left him nothing, no face saving merger, no golden parachute, he deliberately crushed him.

ARICIA: I saw it coming three months before. Your father has people on his team that hate him. I had three calls giving me inside information. I begged my father to protect our position. He wouldn't listen to his daughter. He thought he was a tightrope walker.

WILLIAM *starts to leave.*

Where are you going?

WILLIAM: It's feeding time.

ARICIA: We're never alone.

WILLIAM: I don't think we—

ARICIA: Something's happening to me.

WILLIAM: I need to get to the stables.

ARICIA: It's…never happened before.

WILLIAM: Yes.

ARICIA: Do you know what I mean?

WILLIAM: Please.

Pause.

ARICIA: Please.

WILLIAM: What?

ARICIA: Touch my lips.

WILLIAM *touches her lips, then abruptly leaves. Alone,* ARICIA *touches her lips.*

He touched my lips. He touched my lips.

•

ARICIA *leaves as* FAYE *enters.* WILLIAM *enters.*

WILLIAM: I heard what you tried to do to me.

Pause.

FAYE: You don't understand the reason.

WILLIAM: It's ironic. I was going until I learned you wanted to throw me out of my own house. Then of course I had to stay.

FAYE: You don't understand.

WILLIAM: I'd be so happy—

FAYE: [*overlapping*] He told you?

WILLIAM: —far away from—[you]

FAYE: How could he?!

WILLIAM: He didn't.

FAYE: Then who?

WILLIAM: But I'm not going. [*pause*] Not yet.

WILLIAM *leaves.* FAYE *is alone.*

FAYE: Funny how things stick in the mind: a chair in the sunlight.

THOMAS *enters.*

FAYE: Take off your shirt.

THOMAS: All things come to those who wait?

FAYE: Please.

THOMAS: [*taking his shirt off*] All things.

FAYE: Turn around.

THOMAS: [*turning his back to her*] Okay.

FAYE: [*tracing on his lower back*] Here it is—eleven years ago, and here [*between his shoulder blades*], seventeen.

THOMAS: [*turning, grasping her*] Please.

FAYE *wrenches herself away from him and leaves.* THOMAS *fucks the chair.* NONNY *watches from an unseen distance.*

THOMAS: Strip for me. I wanna hear the crowd get raucous. I want to see the waitress spill the beer. I want to watch you step out of a sea shell. Venus born in a Bourbon Street strip joint. Classy, rattling snare drum. Ass grinding like a jackhammer on my love nerve. Whiskey burns my throat. Pasties, g-string, distant points on a constellation as yet uncharted.

NONNY *clears her throat.* THOMAS *stops.* NONNY *approaches.*

NONNY: Working late?

THOMAS: Yeah.

NONNY *massages* THOMAS' *back.*

THOMAS: Not the back, the neck.

NONNY: All right.

THOMAS: The neck.

NONNY: I'm getting there.

THOMAS: [*screaming*] The neck!

The uproar brings ARICIA *into the doorway where she observes unnoticed.*

NONNY: What's wrong with you?!!

THOMAS: [*perfectly composed*] I had a perfect butler once—humble man. He'd do anything to please me—lick my ass if I wanted. One day I asked for a glass of water, and he brought a bottle of 1938 Taittinger Blanc de Blanc and served it for me in a Tiffany crystal chalice. When he finished pouring I fired him. In order to teach him that pleasure consists not in what I enjoy, but in having my own way.

NONNY: [*offended*] I don't work for you.

THOMAS: Then why are you rubbing me?

NONNY *storms out.* ARICIA *approaches him.*

ARICIA: Poor Thomas, you think of your dicky as a kind of Leviathan, like one of those whales you slaughter on your shipping routes.

THOMAS: I destroyed your father, ate his company and spit out the bones.

ARICIA: True, I hear it's fat, but can it spout like Moby?

THOMAS: Do you know why I took you into my house?

ARICIA: Do you know why I stay?

THOMAS: You're a living souvenir of my greatest deal.

ARICIA: I'm waiting for the right moment.

THOMAS: Snipe all you want from the junk bond pits because that's where you'll stay. I've seen to that, blackballed you on the exchange so you have to suck my charity.

ARICIA: Is that why you want me here? Makes you feel potent?

THOMAS: I want you where I can watch you.

ARICIA: I'm so thirsty.

ARICIA downs glass after glass of water unable to slake her thirst. THOMAS takes the pitcher and leaves.

•

ANGUS is peering around a screen when NONNY enters.

NONNY: What are you doing?

ANGUS: She's in the bath again.

NONNY: I know that.

ANGUS: Always splashing—and always silent.

NONNY: She's afraid of bursting into flames.

ANGUS: Why?

NONNY: She's heard stories.

ANGUS: Could that happen?

NONNY: Someone is watching.

ANGUS: Who?

He turns back to NONNY.

I'm starving.

NONNY: Go eat.

ARICIA strips WILLIAM of his shirt. ANGUS and NONNY watch.

ANGUS: Look at us, still in our formal attire, and no one's had anything to eat but potatoes and tea for weeks.

NONNY: That's a lie.

ANGUS: The cupboard is bare.

NONNY: Gus, we've got to keep this house together.

ANGUS: I'm trying.

NONNY: Stop that girl.

ANGUS: No.

NONNY: She's driving him mad.

ANGUS: Don't blame her.

NONNY: Why not?

ANGUS: The madness is in him.

NONNY: He's a good boy.

ANGUS: A time bomb.

NONNY: How can you say that about him?

ANGUS: I love him.

NONNY: Yeah.

ANGUS: Didn't I teach him everything I know?

NONNY: Yes, Angus.

ANGUS: The poor girl's been shut out like a leper.

NONNY: Bullshit.

ANGUS: I saw her every day as if it were late at night and it was my job to close the cafe.

NONNY: You never worked in a cafe.

ANGUS: And she was locked in an embrace with the last customer in a desperate attempt to make contact—with someone. Anyone. [*pause*]

The Cafe De Flore. Tea. Chocolat. Welsh Rarebit. She was a rare bite.

NONNY: Stop it, you wanker.

ARICIA *leans in to kiss* WILLIAM. THOMAS *enters.*

THOMAS: What's this?

WILLIAM *pulls on his shirt and leaves.*

ARICIA: Your power died centuries ago.

THOMAS: Cross me and you won't walk away.

ARICIA: You're a fossil.

THOMAS: Leave my son alone.

ARICIA: Tell that to him.

THOMAS: Do you like living in this house?

ARICIA: Such a honking sound.

THOMAS: It could be your grave.

ARICIA: I saw a charnel house once at St. Catherine's Monastery. The monks believe it's the place God spoke to Moses from the burning bush. They use a whole building to store the skulls of the monks who've died there. Sixteen centuries worth. I walked into the first room; floor to ceiling skulls. I took it in a long time—how some skulls rested on top of others; one as if embracing; another pressuring about to attack. I never believed a pile of bone could be so expressive. The room seemed alive. I never went back. But this place is just like that charnel house. I'm the burning bush and you're the skull.

FAYE *enters and seems paralyzed. Everyone surrounds her except* ARICIA *who strolls off.*

THOMAS: Faye.

No response.

Faye?

He touches her arm but she shows no recognition. In frustration he follows ARICIA. NONNY *motions for* ANGUS *to leave.*

NONNY: Angus.

ANGUS *leaves.*

NONNY: Where is your husband?

FAYE: He's not here.

NONNY: You know he is.

FAYE: Do you see him?

NONNY: You're deluded.

FAYE: He's never here, he's always vanishing.

NONNY: And when he walks through that door?

FAYE: Maybe he'll forgive me.

NONNY: His last lover is dead. The mother of his—

FAYE: It was self-defense.

NONNY: That was never proven.

FAYE: Are you trying to frighten me?

NONNY: I want you to stop.

FAYE: That's not possible.

NONNY: Can't you see what's going to happen?

FAYE: My eyes are open.

NONNY: Even if you could fool Thomas, you still can't have William. He hates women.

FAYE: Then I've got no competition.

NONNY: You're talking like a fool.

FAYE: I can touch him.

NONNY: He hates you.

FAYE: He's got a wild streak he can't control.

NONNY: So do you.

FAYE: We'll smash into one another.

Pause.

NONNY: [*struggling to control herself*] My sweet girl.

FAYE: What?!

NONNY: What about me?

FAYE: Nothing's going to happen to you.

NONNY: When this destroys you, where will I go?

FAYE: Please—don't.

NONNY: Where?

FAYE: Then there's only one answer.

NONNY: No, stop it.

FAYE: I have to die.

NONNY: No! No! You're just crazed, no!

•

THOMAS: What do you think a larvae is?

ANGUS: It's the earliest stages of an insect, right?

THOMAS: I don't know.

ANGUS: Why?

THOMAS: Don't know, just thinking.

ANGUS: [*getting up*] D' you want anything?

THOMAS: Where are you going?

ANGUS: The kitchen.

THOMAS: Oh.

ANGUS: You all right?

THOMAS: Why?

ANGUS: You seem worried.

THOMAS: Pacific rim.

ANGUS: Is that all?

ARICIA *enters, sees them both and starts to leave.*

THOMAS: Sit down.

ARICIA: [*sitting*] You never cease to amaze me.

ANGUS: I'll be going.

ARICIA: G' night.

THOMAS: Check all the doors.

ANGUS *leaves.*

That advice you gave me paid off better than anything all year. How do you do it?

ARICIA: The basics: observation, analysis, and luck.

THOMAS: It was brilliant.

ARICIA: Thank you.

THOMAS: You have anything else for me?

ARICIA: [*pointedly*] No.

THOMAS: What do you mean, "no"?

ARICIA: Not until I have a completely different contract.

THOMAS: Out of the question.

ARICIA: Do you believe that when a man and a woman are left alone in a room—no matter who they are—they will surely copulate?

THOMAS: No. [*pause*] Do you?

ARICIA: I have trouble with the old stories.

THOMAS: Harsh.

ARICIA: Listen to you.

THOMAS: I can be very gentle.

ARICIA: I read you sleep with your thing in a glove of vaseline.

THOMAS: Myth.

ARICIA: Like everything about you?

THOMAS: No one's more real.

ARICIA: Like a rock, heh?

THOMAS: Why are you always on the attack?

ARICIA: Some day you'll stumble.

THOMAS: You hate me that much.

ARICIA: Not anymore.

THOMAS: I'm disappointed in you.

ARICIA: How so?

THOMAS: I've never known you to lie.

ARICIA: I lie all the time.

THOMAS: You're lying right now.

ARICIA: Perhaps.

THOMAS: I've come to depend on you.

ARICIA: You must be desperate.

THOMAS: Do you think when two people are alone anything can happen?

ARICIA: Yes.

THOMAS: I think it's all very volatile.

ARICIA: Being alone?

THOMAS: Everything.

ARICIA: Can you smell the sulpher and the pitch?

THOMAS: Can you hear the wailing?

ARICIA: [*laughing*] Sometimes you can be very funny.

THOMAS: That's why they pay me the big bucks.

ARICIA: And they are big.

THOMAS: Yes, they are. Do you need more?

ARICIA: Need you ask?

THOMAS: Have you seen Faye?

ARICIA: Yes.

THOMAS: Well?

ARICIA: Well?

THOMAS: Where is she?

ARICIA: In the greenhouse. When I walked through

she was lying naked, face down, writhing in a bed of begonias. She has a rash across her ass—most unattractive—but the pumping she was doing was appealing. She was clawing at the dirt and shoving it beneath her. It was strange, but I think I understood.

THOMAS: I'm afraid I have a meeting.

ARICIA: This late?

THOMAS: It's already midday on the Nikkei.

ARICIA: It is late.

THOMAS: Yes it is.

ARICIA: Very late.

THOMAS: Late.

ARICIA: Yes.

THOMAS: You'll excuse me?

ARICIA: Of course.

THOMAS *walks to the door and turns back to* ARICIA.

THOMAS: Good night.

ARICIA: Good night.

THOMAS: Good night.

ARICIA: Good night.

THOMAS: Good night.

ARICIA: Good night.

THOMAS *leaves.* ARICIA *runs to the threshold, and sinks, head in hands, then slowly stands rejoicing, elation rising on her face.* NONNY *enters urgently.*

NONNY: Where's Thomas?

ARICIA: It's too late.

NONNY: What do you mean?

ARICIA: He's dead.

NONNY: Oh Lord!

THOMAS *speaks at a distance as if in a coma. The others do not hear.*

THOMAS: Yes... [*pause*] There was a—

ARICIA: A call just came.

THOMAS: ...and...

NONNY: Oh my God—Faye—[*pause*] How did it happen?

THOMAS: I've got to get—

ARICIA: They found his car in the river. It went off an embankment. His driver was dead behind the wheel, but they haven't found him yet. He must've been washed down river.

THOMAS: The hounds...

NONNY: Then maybe he's alive.

ARICIA *shakes her head no.*

THOMAS: The hounds of hell snarling...

NONNY: I never thought he could die.

THOMAS: My strength is gone.

ARICIA: Maybe he can't.

NONNY: Don't talk nonsense.

ARICIA: Do you know what this means?

NONNY: No.

ARICIA: The board will choose a new CEO.

NONNY: How can you think about that when—

ARICIA: [*commanding*] Be quiet. [*pause*] Who will it be?

THOMAS: Gotta get back.

ARICIA: Go get Faye.

NONNY *runs to the sleeping* FAYE *and shakes her awake.*

THOMAS: I remember her in Manila during the rainy season. She'd walk along the terrace in a sarong, her tits bare, with one of those pyramidal Chinese hats on her head—huge.

FAYE: Let me go.

THOMAS: The rain would pelt her until the paper fan she carried disintegrated. Then she'd get another fan and continue to defy the monsoon. My cock would stiffen.

FAYE: Let me go.

NONNY: No, listen, I have something to tell you.

FAYE: [*groggy*] Sleep…sleep…

NONNY: Listen! Thomas is dead.

FAYE: What!

THOMAS: Have to get back.

NONNY: Thomas is dead.

FAYE: How do you know this?

NONNY: I'm so sorry.

FAYE: How do you know?!

NONNY: You're free.

FAYE: [*dazed*] Free?

NONNY: Free to love William.

THOMAS: Have to…

FAYE: [*moaning*] Ohhhhh…

NONNY: Let me speak to him for you.

FAYE: No! Let me die.

FAYE *passes out.* NONNY *touches her face.*

NONNY: Never.

As NONNY *leaves,* THOMAS *passes her unseen. Outside* NONNY *discovers* ANGUS.

NONNY: Where were you?

ANGUS: Looking for Aricia.

NONNY: Where?

ANGUS: The greenhouse.

NONNY: You spying again?

Annoyed, he starts to leave. NONNY *catches him.*

Angus?

ANGUS: Yes?

NONNY: Will you…

ANGUS: [*pausing*] Will I what?

NONNY: [*coming closer*] Would you…

She starts to tremble. A horrible resistance builds up in her.

ANGUS: Are you [*pause*] asking…

NONNY: [*pause*] Oh never mind.

ARICIA *enters.*

ANGUS: I've been looking for you.

ARICIA: Yes?

ANGUS: [*to* NONNY] Would you excuse us?

NONNY: Aren't you a little old?

ANGUS: [*waiting*] Well?

NONNY *leaves.*

William needs to talk to you.

ARICIA: I'm afraid to see him.

ANGUS: What about "the challenge?"

ARICIA: Everything's different now.

ANGUS: Why?

ARICIA: Rebelling against his old man excited him. With Thomas dead I'm sure he'll lose interest in me.

ANGUS: You're saying you feel something?

ARICIA: I love him.

ANGUS: I'm astonished.

ARICIA: You insult me.

ANGUS: Forgive me.

ARICIA: [*pausing*] All right.

ANGUS: I know he loves you.

ARICIA: There's nothing I want more.

WILLIAM *enters.*

WILLIAM: I'm meeting with the board, but before I do there's something I have to talk to you about.

He glances at ANGUS *who understands to leave.*

Now that he's dead, I suppose you want to leave?

ARICIA: [*struggling*] Well, I hadn't…

WILLIAM: Every firm wants you, and now there's no one stopping you.

ARICIA: I don't know what to say.

WILLIAM: With your ability you'll make millions, then you'll start your own company.

ARICIA: I see.

WILLIAM: Whatever's happened in this house between you and me is in the past. You're free. I need you to know that.

ARICIA: Thank you, but do you think that's what I want?

WILLIAM: Are you negotiating?

ARICIA: I'm trying to tell you—

WILLIAM: Some on the board want you. They know Faye's unstable, and the old money doesn't want the stigma of a bastard son at the helm. They'd rather claim the glory of healing bad blood, *and* put a financial genius in the chair.

ARICIA: That's hard to believe.

WILLIAM: And I agree with them.

ARICIA: What do you mean?

WILLIAM: If you'll stay, I'll throw my proxy in for you. It'll be your company, and rightfully so.

ARICIA: I'm afraid I'm dreaming.

WILLIAM: Maybe we are.

THOMAS *appears in the distance.*

THOMAS: Have to get back...

ARICIA: You'd give up your own chance for my sake?

WILLIAM: My reason is caving in to something so passionate it's choking me.

ARICIA: Why?

WILLIAM: I don't want to breathe any more except with your breath. For months I've been incapable of showing you what I feel. Struggling to get free from you. I see you everywhere, in the shadows, even in my horses' eyes. Forgive me. Love is so strange to me my words are all mangled. But ugly as they are, every one's a vow. Please don't reject them. Without you I never would have spoken.

ANGUS *enters. In another room* THOMAS *kneels by* FAYE'S *side and caresses his sleeping wife.*

THOMAS: My poor sleeping one, sleep while you can.

ANGUS: Faye wants to see you.

WILLIAM: [*looking at* ARICIA] Tell her I can't. I'm waiting for an answer.

THOMAS: The sap is rising.

ANGUS: You've got no choice.

WILLIAM: Hold her back.

THOMAS: Will you wear the red wig? Will you ride the bright lights? Will you do it with the peacocks around us?

ARICIA: Let her come. [*pause*] I accept all your offers.

THOMAS: Will you love me?

As ARICIA *leaves,* FAYE *rises,* THOMAS *fades away, and* FAYE *walks through a maze to* WILLIAM.

FAYE: I found you.

WILLIAM: Yes, you've quite a nose.

FAYE: I can't banter today. [*to* ANGUS] Would you excuse us?

WILLIAM: No.

FAYE: [*commanding*] Angus.

ANGUS *leaves.*

I know you must hate me, and I understand, I've given you every reason.

WILLIAM: What makes you say that?

FAYE: Please don't patronize me. I've come to ask for your help.

WILLIAM: What a droll wit.

FAYE: Not for me, for my sons. I'm not going to live much longer, and with Thomas dead I know the board will eliminate my boys. And because I've made you an enemy I'm afraid you'll turn your anger on them.

WILLIAM: I don't feel anything like that.

FAYE: It's only natural that you would, the things I've done to you. But you didn't know the real reason why.

WILLIAM: Oh, but I do.

FAYE: [*pause*] Really? [*pause as he looks away*] Do you?

FAYE *approaches* WILLIAM. *He backs away.*

FAYE: You have to face me.

WILLIAM: Why?

FAYE: Your father's dead.

WILLIAM: [*casually*] He always has been.

FAYE: Don't joke about death.

WILLIAM: So what's changed?

FAYE: There's nothing stopping us.

WILLIAM: Did he?

FAYE: Yes.

WILLIAM: Interesting.

FAYE: [*exploding*] Don't stand there with your damn cold mask and pretend you feel nothing!

WILLIAM: I don't wear a mask. That's why I'm offensive to people like you—I say what I think.

FAYE: You're hiding right now.

WILLIAM: Just what am I hiding, "Mother?"

FAYE: Don't call me that!

WILLIAM: *You're* hiding! You'd like to cut my throat.

FAYE: No, I want to stroke it. And that's what you want.

WILLIAM: So says my father's merry widow.

FAYE: I can break down your walls.

WILLIAM: Is that a challenge?

FAYE: Yes.

WILLIAM: A sexual challenge?

FAYE: Yes.

WILLIAM: How titilating.

FAYE: There's a bottle of grain alcohol in the cabinet. One hundred and ninety proof—one of the ways Thomas got his manly laughs. If you give me half an hour with that bottle I'll show you what you really want.

WILLIAM: That stuff's poison!

FAYE: Are you afraid?

WILLIAM: Of what?

FAYE: Me?

WILLIAM: It can make you blind.

FAYE: That's what you are now. Shall I get the bottle?

WILLIAM: After this you'll let me alone?

FAYE: If that's what you want.

WILLIAM: It's a small price—get it.

FAYE *gets the bottle and two shot glasses. She opens and pours as they speak.*

FAYE: This is pleasant.

WILLIAM: The end's in sight.

FAYE: [*teasing*] It will be.

WILLIAM: Look at the name of this stuff!

FAYE: [*laughing, reading*] "Graves."

WILLIAM: Doesn't that make you uneasy?

FAYE: It's where I'll be if I can't have you.

WILLIAM: I'll warn you—

FAYE: Please do.

WILLIAM: I've never been drunk.

FAYE: You've never had me.

WILLIAM *picking up his glass.*

WILLIAM: Shall we?

FAYE: [*toasting*] Love moves.

WILLIAM: [*toasting*] To the hunt.

FAYE: For the secret soul.

They drink. Both react to their innards in flames.

WILLIAM: Ahhhhhhhhhhhhhhhh!

FAYE: [*gasping*] Yes—yes—yes!

WILLIAM: [*not quite recovered*] Must taste a lot...like love.

FAYE: Like fire.

WILLIAM: Like death.

FAYE: Pour another.

He pours two more shots.

WILLIAM: Are you having "a good time?"

FAYE: Oh yes. Are you?

WILLIAM: I'm intrigued.

FAYE: [*toasting*] To your sweet cock.

They drink.

WILLIAM: [*gasping, laughing*] May it ever wave.

FAYE: [*laughing gayly*] See? Something's happening.

WILLIAM: Always is.

FAYE: Did you know that people have a sexual thought every twelve seconds?

WILLIAM: If that's true about your kind, you're in worse pain than I thought.

FAYE: Pour another and you'll feel it.

WILLIAM: I think you're drunk.

FAYE: I became drunk the first time I saw you. Do you remember? You embraced me.

WILLIAM: Humoring my father.

FAYE: I touched your [*groping for the word*]...cheek! [*laughing happily that she found it*] I couldn't remember the word for the part of you that I...that I...touched. So many parts of you—so many small innocent touches—walking to the table...brushing up against your sleeve...would make me tingle. Could you tell? Could you, could you...

Rather than getting drunk, WILLIAM *becomes more precise, more fluid, as if he is rising above his body.*

WILLIAM: I've always been acutely aware of people's unconscious signals.

FAYE: So you knew?

WILLIAM: Yes.

FAYE: So do you think twelve people think of sex every... [*groping for the sense, and laughing*] no, that's not it. So you knew?

WILLIAM: [*laughing*] And I knew that you knew that I knew.

FAYE: You're so charming when you laugh.

WILLIAM: That's not a laugh.

FAYE: Oh you want to quibble?

WILLIAM: Qui?

FAYE: [*whirligigging*] A quibble. A quibble on a quim. A quibble is a pun. Would you like to hear a quibble on a quim? Would that be fun? What would you like to hear? Dear? A quim on a quibble?

WILLIAM: No.

FAYE: So how much did you know? Everything?

WILLIAM: Yes.

FAYE: We don't have to talk then, do we?

WILLIAM: I'd like that.

FAYE: So would I.

They stare at one another in silence.

FAYE: Are you a virgin?

WILLIAM: Isn't everyone?

FAYE: I've got children.

WILLIAM: Contact between two people is an illusion.

FAYE: Then how'd I conceive two sons?

WILLIAM: You wanted it so badly you dreamt it.

FAYE: Then let me dream again.

WILLIAM: You are.

FAYE: Then dance with me.

WILLIAM: We are.

FAYE: We're not moving.

WILLIAM: The dance is in the eyes.

FAYE: For someone who doesn't believe in love, you're very—

WILLIAM: Lie down.

FAYE: All right.

WILLIAM: Spread your arms.

FAYE: Like so?

WILLIAM: [*standing over her*] Can you feel the distance between us?

FAYE: Yes.

WILLIAM: It will never go away.

FAYE: Lie next to me.

He does.

WILLIAM: [*deliberately*] Take my hand.

She does.

FAYE: Do you feel what's passing through our fingers?

WILLIAM: Bite my hand.

She does. WILLIAM *gasps in pain. He rises calmly and drives his point home.*

Understand that you have never *touched* me.

FAYE *rises.*

FAYE: Pour another.

WILLIAM: You're drunk enough.

FAYE: Are you?

WILLIAM: I warned you.

FAYE: [*trying to control herself*] You made a deal!

WILLIAM: Fine.

WILLIAM *pours two more shots, and they drink.*

FAYE: Ohhhh, it goes right through me!

WILLIAM: Almost pure.

FAYE: Like you—almost.

WILLIAM: It reminds me of riding.

FAYE: Would you like to go riding?

WILLIAM: [*a little distant*] I already am.

FAYE: You can ride me.

WILLIAM: I knew I wasn't ready to ride the dappled mare, but she's so beautiful.

FAYE: Mount me.

WILLIAM: She's never been ridden. She's angry.

FAYE: I'll do anything you want.

WILLIAM: She takes me deep into the woods, and starts trying to scrape me off by rubbing up against these sharp pines, and running under low tree limbs.

FAYE: I'll get down on my hands and knees and spread my ass for you.

WILLIAM: That doesn't work so she starts back to the stables, I can't stop her, she's so strong.

FAYE: I'll lie on my back and drink your come all night.

WILLIAM: She's running along a logging road, there's a deep ditch along one side. I'm trying to get control with the reins. I'm pulling so hard I've got her head pulled back all the way to her right side—she's running hard without even looking where she's going. I think if I keep this up I might topple us both into the ditch. I could be killed.

FAYE: I'll bathe your whole body with my juices.

WILLIAM: I have to let go to save us both. So I do.

FAYE: I'll do anything...anything...

WILLIAM: What an amazing feeling, she takes off at a full gallop. I'm on a runaway.

FAYE: Anything.

WILLIAM: Nothing's ever felt as good as that wild ride completely out of control, wind streaming in my eyes, tears running down my face, mare panting, the foam rising on her flanks…

FAYE: [*imploring*] William…

WILLIAM: [*rising*] Thank you for the drink. I have to go.

FAYE: [*breaking down, crying to heaven*] Oh help me! Please, help me, please…

WILLIAM *hears* ANGUS *returning.*

WILLIAM: You'd better leave.

FAYE: I'll never give up.

WILLIAM: You don't want to be seen this way.

She runs out. ANGUS *enters.*

Act Two

ANGUS: Why's she running?

WILLIAM *won't answer.*

Why are you so flushed?

WILLIAM *is silent.*

I see.

WILLIAM *approaches* ANGUS *but stops, unable to move.* ANGUS *offers his arms.*

Come here.

WILLIAM *folds into his arms.*

WILLIAM: Just hold me.

ANGUS: My dear boy.

Long pause.

I came to tell you I heard the board has chosen Faye as the new chair.

WILLIAM *leaps up in anger and springs toward the door.*

WILLIAM: They can't do that!

ANGUS: [*blocking him*] They've done it.

WILLIAM: I'll change it.

ANGUS: I thought you wanted no part of it.

WILLIAM: Things are different now.

ANGUS: Before you do something rash, there's a rumor that your father's been sighted.

WILLIAM: What! No, that son of a bitch can't come back from the dead!

ANGUS: It's just a rumor, but I never underestimate your father.

WILLIAM: First we kill the rumor, then we call an emergency board meeting. I told Aricia I'd give her control.

ANGUS: You have changed.

•

NONNY: The smartest thing for us to do is to take the children and leave...get as far from him as we—

FAYE: [*enraged*] I can't leave him.

NONNY: You sound like your mother! You'll forget everything, even your children, for this insanity?!

FAYE: You encouraged me!

NONNY: I didn't!

FAYE: You made me believe he could love me.

NONNY: Maybe I did, but there's nothing I wouldn't do to save you from this.

FAYE: I would've died silent, you pried all this out of me. Now you tell me I should run!

NONNY: Yes!

FAYE: I should have run from you!

NONNY: You don't even know what you're saying.

FAYE: I want you to go to him and offer him anything.

The chairmanship, I'll step aside. Get down on your knees and beg, but get him for me.

NONNY: I don't know...how.

FAYE: Do it. I'll wait for you. Go on.

NONNY *leaves. Unseen,* ARICIA *watches* FAYE.

FAYE: Whoever—whatever—you are that's doing this to me, please stop. In my dreams he comes to me—not night after night—that'd be too predictible, I could fortify myself. No, he waits until I'm mourning for him and then he makes love to me. He always sits in that chair before he leaves. In the sunlight. And the dust swooning in the beams of light is laden with the scent of our love. It fades when I wake and see Thomas. And I realize I'm not married to the light. I'm bound to a man whose every thought is a conscious act. Then nights go by, and I wait. In the desert. Finally he comes. And our flesh mingles and our minds meld, and my whole being floats into him, and he takes residence in me, and I have an overwhelming feeling of arrival. My parched lungs drink deep and long wet breaths of salt air. But I can't anymore, I can't...I can't...

Whatever you are—why destroy me? I know you want to punish William. Then make him love me. Wouldn't that be revenge? Make him love me.

ARICIA *steps out of the shadows.*

ARICIA: What if that's impossible?

Startled, FAYE *turns away.*

Why do you avoid me?

FAYE *looks at her with scorn.*

That could change.

FAYE: How?

ARICIA *moves to within inches of* FAYE. *They study one another.*

ARICIA: Let me quench you.

Slowly, ARICIA *moves to kiss* FAYE. FAYE *almost responds then pushes her away.* FAYE *leaves.* ARICIA *is alone. Light strikes the chair. She sits, almost motionless.*

•

NONNY *enters the sitting room where the rest of the household, gathered around a funeral wreath, is holding a wake for* THOMAS.

ARICIA: Shouldn't she be here?

NONNY: She's not well.

ARICIA: No restraint.

NONNY: Hold your tongue!

ANGUS: Nonny.

NONNY: Don't Nonny me…certain things—

ANGUS: [*pointedly*] The occasion.

NONNY *takes a moment to recover, then turns to* WILLIAM.

NONNY: May I speak to you for a moment—alone?

WILLIAM: [*ignoring her*] Does anyone know any jokes?

NONNY: I don't think this is the time.

WILLIAM: It's a wake isn't it?

ARICIA: Have you heard the one about the guy named Joe Dick?

WILLIAM: No.

ANGUS: No.

ARICIA: Growing up was hell, a constant humilation, so when he left home he decided to change his name. [*pause*] To Bob Dick.

NONNY *erupts with laughter.*

NONNY: Oh that's funny! Bob Dick! Oh, Oh, Oh, that's funny.

She clutches the wreath and tries to stop laughing.

Ha, ha, I have to stop laughing, it's not right, ha, ha, ha, ha, no I must stop, ha, ha, please someone help me, ha, ha, ha, Bob Dick! ha, ha, no, help me.

No one moves because THOMAS *enters, as if from the dead, drenched and disheveled. They stare stunned.* NONNY'S *laughter chokes and she reels away.*

•

FAYE *senses* NONNY *returning.*

FAYE: No, too soon, too soon.

NONNY *enters.*

Too soon.

NONNY: Thomas.

FAYE: No.

NONNY: He's alive.

FAYE: He'll find out what I've done.

NONNY: Yes he will.

Long pause.

FAYE: [*attacking*] Why would you want to hurt me?!

NONNY: I'd never hurt you.

FAYE: I was ready to die. My offending parts were already below the earth. And you dragged me up. Why?

NONNY: How can you blame me for wanting you to live?

FAYE: I was going to die with my name clean. Now I'm going to die a whore! And you're the reason.

NONNY: Don't you dare put this off on me. You loved him. You went after him.

FAYE: I never would have.

NONNY: Don't make me your scapegoat.

FAYE: William...you'll enjoy this.

NONNY: What if he doesn't say anything?

FAYE: Don't start twisting again.

NONNY: No, I don't think he will.

FAYE: Even if he doesn't, it'll all be clear to Thomas. This time I'll find a faster way to die. Don't stop me again.

NONNY: You'll give your boys a mother who killed herself for lust?

FAYE: [*breaking*] No!

NONNY: How could you?

FAYE: Please, no, I don't want to hurt them.

NONNY: Well?

FAYE: That's the only thing I regret.

NONNY: Then attack William before he attacks you. Let me tell Thomas he tried to rape you.

FAYE: NO!

NONNY: It makes me sick too, but this is not the time for—

FAYE: I can't put him in that danger.

NONNY: His father loves him—in his way. He won't really hurt him, he'll just drive him out, and he deserves that.

FAYE: I couldn't get those words out of my mouth.

NONNY: All I need is for you to be silent.

FAYE: I can't absorb any more guilt.

NONNY: [*lashing out*] It's not just for you. It's for your boys. Don't destroy them by indulging your self pity. William wants to crush you. Be brutal and help them survive. That's what a mother does!

FAYE: I don't know anything anymore. I'm completely out of control. Do what you will.

NONNY *leaves. Outside the door,* ANGUS *waits for her and takes her arm.*

ANGUS: Nonny.

NONNY: It's late.

ANGUS: Too late to tend the garden.

NONNY: The dark's a good time.

ANGUS: I'll do it in the morning.

NONNY: What if there is no morning?

ANGUS: Touch me.

NONNY: Good gracious, no.

THOMAS *enters.* FAYE *sits almost without reaction. He offers his hand. She rises and takes it quietly.*

THOMAS: Faye.

She doesn't respond.

Faye?

No response. WILLIAM *enters.*

WILLIAM: Father.

THOMAS: Later.

WILLIAM: Father. Aricia and—

THOMAS: Leave us alone.

WILLIAM *withdraws.*

Is this the welcome I get? I've been away a long time. Can you tell me what's wrong?

She removes her hand, wanders away, and starts a drifting dance.

Would you like some tea?

She stops dancing.

THOMAS: When you don't listen…

FAYE: Ummm?

THOMAS: I'm lost.

FAYE: Fine, I'll have some tea.

THOMAS: That's not the point.

FAYE: I'll make it.

THOMAS: It's already made.

FAYE: Are the cups full?

THOMAS: Spilling over the rim.

FAYE: Hmmmmmm…

THOMAS: I'll get the tea—

FAYE: We never used to drink tea.

THOMAS: I know that. [*pause as he gazes at her*] I'm having a miniature stage built for you in the bedroom.

FAYE: Why?

THOMAS: So that you can perform.

FAYE: *Hire* the talent.

THOMAS: No one else will do what I need.

FAYE: I can't.

ARICIA *appears in the open doorway.*

THOMAS: What's happened to you?

FAYE: Ummm?

THOMAS: It's as if you're disappearing.

FAYE: Maybe I am.

THOMAS: Do you want me to inform the board?

FAYE: No business after dinner, remember?

THOMAS: They'll divy your shares like party favors.

FAYE: When you were gone…

THOMAS: [*pause*] Yeah?

FAYE: Something horrible happened.

THOMAS: What?

FAYE: [*leaving*] You won't see me.

THOMAS: What's this all about?

FAYE *walks out.* THOMAS *notices* ARICIA *who slips away.*

•

FAYE *waits until* WILLIAM *is asleep, then cuts a lock of his hair. After she leaves he wakes and feels for the missing hair. He panics and starts screaming.*

WILLIAM: Goddammit, you fucking bastard, you cocksucking son of a bitch, you freak fucking dog raper, you—Ohhhhhhhhhhh—you goddam—ohhhh—Nooooo—

THOMAS *rushes in and grabs* WILLIAM, *shaking him to stop.*

THOMAS: William!

WILLIAM: Stop!

THOMAS: Snap out of it!

WILLIAM: Stop!

THOMAS: You're all right, it's just a dream!

WILLIAM: Get away from me.

THOMAS: Goddammit, get a grip.

WILLIAM *begins to ease, breathing heavily.*

WILLIAM: What are you doing?

THOMAS: I heard you screaming, I ran in.

WILLIAM: I'm fine now, you can go.

THOMAS: Why don't you tell me what this was about.

WILLIAM: Why?

THOMAS: What the hell went on when I was gone?

WILLIAM: A boy stood outside the house every single day. He had his hands over his eyes.

THOMAS: I want to know what happened to Faye.

WILLIAM: I can't be near that woman any more.

THOMAS: Why?

WILLIAM: What do you want?

THOMAS: I want to help you.

WILLIAM: What do you want?

THOMAS: Is that all you can you say?

WILLIAM: Well?

THOMAS: I want to talk.

WILLIAM: Why?

THOMAS: Every time we talk nothing gets said.

WILLIAM: Because nothing you say has anything to do with who you are.

THOMAS: [*temper rising*] Boy—who I am you'll never know.

WILLIAM: You're transparent.

THOMAS: No, you can't see me, I'm never in the same place twice.

WILLIAM: I know you by what you do, and that woman you brought into this house is twisted.

THOMAS: I had a stepmother too. She was a piece 'a work: a piece of ass, but a piece 'a poison. So I know what you're going through.

WILLIAM: Ah, the sympathetic father.

THOMAS: One of many faces, all true. Some people call me a demon, others a machine; I kinda like that one—a fornicating machine.

WILLIAM: With a long line of people waiting with their death wish in their sweaty palms.

THOMAS: [*like a laser*] Now you've made me very angry.

ARICIA *appears in the door and witnesses* THOMAS *drive* WILLIAM *away with his gaze.*

ARICIA: I saw what you did to your son.

THOMAS: Oh?

ARICIA: Do you want to watch a private act?

THOMAS: [*whispering*] Yes.

ARICIA: [*forcing him to say it louder*] What?

THOMAS: Yes.

ARICIA *sits at the table, and, pouring water from a*

pitcher, downs glass after glass of water, unable to slake her thirst.

ARICIA: I feel love's raging thirst.

She rubs her hands in the water spilled on the table top, lifts her dress slightly and rubs the water on the insides of her thighs. THOMAS *stands behind her, and breathes in deeply.*

THOMAS: What do you want?

ARICIA: A place on the board.

THOMAS: Fine.

ARICIA: Twenty percent of the shares.

THOMAS: Shall we?

ARICIA: Yes, let's.

They do not move. A long pause. NONNY *enters and stares at them transfixed.* ARICIA *leaves.*

•

In another room WILLIAM *shakes violently like a sapling in a fierce wind.*

•

THOMAS: You're saying he tried to rape her?

NONNY: Yes.

THOMAS: And she's staying silent about it?

NONNY: Yes.

THOMAS: That son of a bitch, I'll kill him. You have proof?

NONNY: Why do you think she fought so hard to send him away? This has been brewing since he first saw her.

THOMAS: It doesn't make sense. Why didn't she say anything?

NONNY: To protect you. She was ashamed.

THOMAS: I can't believe it! I'll kill him.

NONNY: I have to go—I'm afraid to leave her alone.

•

WILLIAM: Do you think she's crazy enough to tell him what she's done?

ANGUS: Yes. You have to tell him first.

WILLIAM: [*vehemently*] No.

ANGUS: Why not?

WILLIAM *won't answer.*

I see. [*pause*]

WILLIAM: Stop it! [*pause*] I was about to tell him about Aricia.

ANGUS: Don't.

WILLIAM *stares at* ANGUS *in disbelief.*

Just take her and go.

WILLIAM *starts to leave.*

WILLIAM: [*turning back*] No. First I've got something to prove.

WILLIAM *finds his way to* THOMAS.

THOMAS: You've got horse shit on your boots.

WILLIAM: I was working in the paddock.

THOMAS: You're going to stink up the whole place.

WILLIAM: The servants will get it. There's something I have to tell you.

THOMAS: Good, I've been wanting to talk with you too.

WILLIAM: Forget it.

THOMAS: I want you to take over the company when I'm gone.

WILLIAM: Forget it.

THOMAS: God dammit, you can't spend your whole life racing horses, boy. Grow up and be a man.

WILLIAM: Like you.

THOMAS: Yes.

WILLIAM: A whoremonger.

THOMAS: You're disgusting.

WILLIAM: You're a feeder—a pirana—

THOMAS: That's enough!

WILLIAM: With your mergers and your hostile takeovers, but mostly you feed on women. Talk about disgusting! Your lechery hangs off your face as plain as a dog's hard on.

THOMAS: Power needs to be fed. I get very hungry. I give my body what it needs. You'll understand someday.

WILLIAM: Will I understand what you did to my mother?

THOMAS: [*blowing up*] She came after me, I had no—

WILLIAM: And Faye's sister—

THOMAS: You don't know what hap—

WILLIAM: And countless others. I could never live up to your reputation. You're legendary, the Great Cocksman.

THOMAS: Doesn't anyone, anything, move you?

WILLIAM: Yes. I love riding into the tempest sweet sixteen sheets to the wind. Winding around the maypole of the Marquis. Flashflooding the assflooding, and lots of ass, beautiful round asses, and lots of ash, beautiful black coal ash, and the ash raining on the ass.

The labyrinth is a delight, but such a tedious habit. What could it mean? This throbbing of desire. It's a malignant accident of nature. I don't want it.

THOMAS: You're strange.

WILLIAM: You need to see what strange is.

THOMAS: A man that can't love is like a man without an ass.

WILLIAM: How delicate.

THOMAS: Ya can't sit, ya can't shit, you're not fit for livin'.

WILLIAM: You're vulgar.

THOMAS: But I can love.

WILLIAM: Bravissimo.

THOMAS: I understand you tried to rape my wife.

WILLIAM: What!

THOMAS: The virgin finally pulls out his chainsaw *in my bed.*

WILLIAM: [*shouting*] That's a lie!

THOMAS: Which part? The virgin?

WILLIAM: I never touched her!

THOMAS: You expect me to believe you! You sick fuck!

WILLIAM: I love Aricia.

THOMAS: Just another lie to cover yourself. You never loved anyone. And now you're a dead man!

WILLIAM: Listen to me!

THOMAS: Get out! I don't want your corpse in my house.

WILLIAM: How can you believe her? Look at her mother! You know who she came from—

ANGUS *enters to investigate the shouting and watches aghast.*

THOMAS: [*raising his hand*] Shut up before I kill you myself! Won't anyone rid me of this scum?!! Please, someone crush him!

WILLIAM: It's in her blood.

THOMAS: GET OUT!

WILLIAM *leaves. Pause.*

THOMAS: I'm going to grind his body into powder.

Pause.

How can I kill my own son?

Pause.

How could I have fathered such a degenerate?

FAYE *enters.* ANGUS *slips away.*

FAYE: I have to…speak to—

THOMAS: Were you listening to me?

FAYE: I have something I need to tell you.

THOMAS: Not now.

FAYE: Please.

THOMAS: NO!

Pause.

FAYE: Thomas.

THOMAS: Do you ever find yourself glancing at animals? At their sexual parts?

FAYE: No.

THOMAS: There was a stallion in the south of Ireland that was awe-inspiring, downright humbling.

FAYE: Have you ever considered that talking about it kills the mystery?

THOMAS: Come here. [*pause*] Please.

FAYE *comes close. He gently squeezes her arms.*

I can't kill it. Do you remember why you married me?

FAYE: [*with difficulty*] Yes.

THOMAS: This mystery—I pretend I'm trying to expose it. It's a game. I know I'll never succeed. And by failing, I pay homage to its power. But when I want to tap its power I say nothing. I let the distance between us call out.

FAYE: [*almost remembering*] Thomas...?

THOMAS: Your eyes call me across oceans. I get so lost in your eyes. Then I'm filled with a longing, your voice singing *come home.*

FAYE: [*becoming aroused*] Home...

THOMAS: You are that home.

FAYE: Hmmmm...

THOMAS: And I desire to make a journey.

FAYE: Home.

THOMAS: I have to navigate. Storms rise. The old salts say the seventh wave is the worst, the one that does the damage.

FAYE: My heart is so damaged.

THOMAS: I know. That makes my desire almost unbearable.

FAYE: Yes.

THOMAS: And I say your name over and over, Faye… Faye…

FAYE: [*putting her finger to his lips*] Shhhh…

THOMAS: And your eyes…Beacons.

FAYE: Shhhh…

THOMAS: Draw me home.

FAYE: Shhhh…

THOMAS: With your eyes.

Their lips come close, sensing without motion. Finally, FAYE *breaks away.*

FAYE: Don't threaten William, please. Call off what you've…

THOMAS: How can you defend him after what he's done to you?

FAYE: He's innocent.

THOMAS: No one is.

FAYE: Please!

THOMAS: He's a liar. And a good one.

FAYE: No! Listen to me—

THOMAS: He knows if you have to lie make it a big one. So the son of a bitch has cooked up the biggest lie of his life—he claims he loves Aricia.

Long pause.

FAYE: What?

THOMAS: You heard me—that's a laugh—him love anyone!

FAYE *turns away.* THOMAS *tries to hold her. She stiffens. He leaves.*

FAYE: He loves her. [*pause*] No. I can't save him.

FAYE *presses her palms against the door as if to hold back what's outside.*

FAYE: How can he want her over me?

NONNY *enters.*

NONNY: How do you know it's true?

FAYE: You've known all along, haven't you?

NONNY *turns away silent.*

I want her out of this house! I'll rip her apart. No, worse. I'll make her a leper. I'll tell Thomas she's been selling company secrets. He'll squeeze the life from her throat—

No! What am I doing?! It's so twisted. Using my husband to destroy my competition for his son. I've lost my mind!

NONNY: Stop it!

FAYE: I'm disgusting! The woman's innocent—she's never done anything to me, and I want to crucify her.

NONNY: You can't help yourself.

FAYE: I'm loathsome. Crawling with lust so thick I'm no longer human!

NONNY: Stop thinking about your body.

FAYE: It's not my *body* that oozes with desire. It's my mind...

NONNY: Think of other things.

FAYE *searches* NONNY'S *face with her fingers as if she were exploring the features of a lover.*

FAYE: And it hardly seems like *my* mind. The genitalia

of a gargoyle would be more like it. Horribly ugly with its scaly labia, but at the same time sensual and unbearably beautiful, the fleshy folds as innocent as a newborn's. And this thing, it's disembodied, adrift somewhere, maybe everywhere where fluids flow. It knows me, this thing. It touches me, whispers in my ear: "Know him, you must know him."

As if in a trance, FAYE *starts moving towards* WILLIAM. NONNY *understands what is happening and tries to stop her, holding onto her arm to restrain her.* FAYE *is too powerful and tears away.*

NONNY: Nooooo...

FAYE *follows the voice through a maze until she reaches* WILLIAM.

WILLIAM: I have nothing else to say.

FAYE: I know who you really are.

WILLIAM: Impossible.

FAYE: I've been in your room.

WILLIAM: When? I don't believe you.

FAYE: I opened the suitcase under your bed.

WILLIAM: You're bluffing.

FAYE: This is delicious.

WILLIAM: It's locked.

FAYE: I thought it would be exciting to slip my hand into one of your riding gloves, and what did I find?

She holds up a key.

WILLIAM: [*enraged*] Goddammit!

FAYE: Are they your drawings?

WILLIAM: You had no right!

FAYE: The sketch of the woman bending over spreading her cheeks was quite well rendered—the crosshatching was positively salacious.

FAYE *tries to embrace him. He pushes her away. She pummels his chest with her fists until she knocks him down. Then she mounts him.*

FAYE: Why are you like this?!

WILLIAM: I want you to leave me alone!

FAYE: Grind your hips!

WILLIAM: No!

FAYE: Yes!

WILLIAM: Bitch! I hate you!

FAYE: NO, NO, NO, NO—WHY?!

WILLIAM: Get off me!

FAYE: Why are you like this?

WILLIAM: Get off!

FAYE: [*starting to strangle him*] Why?

WILLIAM: No!

FAYE: Yes!

WILLIAM: [*gasping for breath*] You're...chok-ing...

FAYE: Why?!

WILLIAM: My old man—

FAYE: Why?

WILLIAM: My old—

FAYE: Forget about him!

WILLIAM: My old man's a—

FAYE: This is about us—forget him!

WILLIAM: He's—

FAYE: Why!

WILLIAM: He's a—

FAYE: Stop it! Tell me why!

WILLIAM: He's a rapist!

FAYE: NO!

WILLIAM: RAPIST!

FAYE: NO!

WILLIAM: I'm made of rape!

FAYE: NO! Not true!

WILLIAM: Sex makes me sick!

She rolls off him and clutches her belly, moaning. Before he leaves he sits on the chair and watches her for a moment. After he's gone she crawls to the chair and lays her cheek where he was sitting. NONNY *enters, sees her condition, and runs to her.*

NONNY: What happened?

FAYE: He ripped me again.

NONNY: Everyone's a victim of love. Do you think you're the only one? You have to accept it.

FAYE: [*in a dark fury*] Are you still giving me advice? You're the one who accused him of rape. That'll be his death! Get out of—

NONNY: But I was—

FAYE: Get out of this house! I'll give you one hour to pack. Then I never want to see you again. I hope your tongue prattles and shakes in hell!

FAYE *leaves.* NONNY *is alone.*

NONNY: Oh God! To save her, I did everything. And I

lost everything. And this is my reward. [*pause*] Well deserved…

She surveys the room one last time.

All quiet now.

Flesh is just flesh. The wind will blow a curtain. Thread will unravel. Light strikes the table.

She retrieves her hidden bottle, but hesitates before drinking.

No—won't do…

She begins searching the room.

She had some pills.

She finds them and holds the bottle up to the light, measuring.

There…that oughta do. [*laughing ruefully*] The fleas leap from their bags…

She leaves slowly, with a purpose, murmuring.

Well deserved…well deserved…

•

ARICIA *finds* WILLIAM *curled up on the floor.*

ARICIA: Why don't you tell your father the truth?

He can't respond.

You told me you never touched her. Is that the truth?

Silence.

Why can't you speak?

He shakes his head—he doesn't know. She lifts her dress. He thrashes out with his arm commanding her to stop. But he can't cry out, and he can't look away because his eyes desire to know.

Why don't you close your eyes?

She lifts her dress higher.

WILLIAM: [*to the distance*] There it is. The mons veneris. The slit gleaming with moisture, glowing, radiant, larger than life.

She starts to subtly undulate her hips.

I am lost. My gaze is paralyzed. And I'm already many many years away.

She's frozen me. Though my cock has hardened to steel, pulsing visibly, larger than life, I cannot move.

She goes to him, kneels by his side, and lovingly caresses his face.

ARICIA: I love you. But I don't know how much longer I can wait. You'll drown me.

•

FAYE: Nonny, draw me a bath.

There is no answer.

Nonny!

•

ARICIA: William and I are leaving.

THOMAS: He says he loves you.

ARICIA: He does.

THOMAS: Don't trust him. He's dangerous.

ARICIA: You don't know him at all, do you?

THOMAS: He tried to rape my wife!

ARICIA: How can you believe that? Because that's what you'd do?

THOMAS: I have a witness.

ARICIA: A self-serving liar.

THOMAS: And I have Faye's tears. She's been trying to kill herself.

ARICIA: Call it off before you kill the wrong one.

THOMAS: Shut up!

ARICIA: Thomas—the great slayer of monsters. But they're not all dead. [*stopping herself*] But I can't say any more. [*leaving*] We're leaving.

THOMAS: Wait!

She's gone.

What're you saying? [*crying out*] AHHHH! [*pause*] My boy…I have a bad feeling. [*shouting*] Is *everyone* lying?!

He sets out determined to question NONNY.

Where is that old woman? NONNY!

•

ANGUS *moves stealthily to the screen enclosing* FAYE'S *bath. As he peers around the corner he gasps and runs in.*

ANGUS: NONNY!

We hear the sounds of him trying to pull her out of the bathtub.

NO! NO! you sweet thing…NOOO…Come to me…come to me…come to me… ohhhhhhhhh…

•

ARICIA: William is dead.

THOMAS: What!

ARICIA: Your son is dead.

THOMAS: You're lying.

ARICIA: You did it.

THOMAS: No.

ARICIA: Yes.

THOMAS: I said no.

ARICIA: I say yes.

THOMAS: I called it off.

ARICIA: I was there.

THOMAS: It can't be.

ARICIA: They're bringing his body here.

THOMAS: What happened?

ARICIA: He was riding the dappled mare along the shore. Back and forth like a madman. I kept shouting at him to stop. The horse went berserk. She was trying to run out to sea. He fought to control her but she threw him, and he got tangled in the reins. She trampled him to get free. And then they came. His horses...pounding through the surf. All of them. Churning and crashing blind. Their hooves tore him to pieces and they were gone.

THOMAS: Please—NO—please...

ANGUS *enters in a fury.*

ANGUS: You fucking monster!

THOMAS: Get back!

ANGUS: You did it!

THOMAS: Yes.

ANGUS: I'm going to tell the world everything I know about you, your bribes, your extortions, the corpses you leave in immaculate rooms.

THOMAS: Your body will drop away.

ANGUS *goes to strike* THOMAS.

Wither and turn to dust.

ANGUS *hesitates.*

Think again.

ANGUS *storms out of the room.* ARICIA *follows.*

THOMAS: [*grief-stricken*] Oh William, my poor poor boy, somewhere in your twisted soul was a bright light, and I could never gather it. I was always far away. But loved you. I did. [*lashing out*] I didn't want this! How could it happen? I didn't want it!

FAYE *enters.*

FAYE: Thomas?

THOMAS: William's dead.

FAYE: Yes.

THOMAS: I don't know what happened between you, but I'm taking your word because I can't take any more pain.

FAYE: There is no more than this. He was innocent.

THOMAS: You're crueler than life itself.

FAYE: Something beyond me drove me, and with the help of my most loving friend…I…

FAYE *starts swaying as if trying to do her yearning dance, but her body is wracked with tiny convulsions.*

THOMAS: What're you doing?

FAYE: I took poison.

Pause.

THOMAS: Would you like some tea?

FAYE: Did you hear me?

THOMAS: I'll help you to bed.

FAYE: I don't have much time.

THOMAS: That's always the case.

FAYE: Do you understand?!!

THOMAS: No.

FAYE: I'm dying.

THOMAS: Yes.

FAYE: [*faintly*] Going…

Long pause.

THOMAS: You were gone suddenly, out of my hands.

FAYE *approaches the chair.*

FAYE: And now I feel my trembling knees give way.

Her breathing becomes serene, then she sinks to her knees, clutching the chair.

ARICIA *enters. She and* THOMAS *lock eyes.*

THE END

AMERICAN THEATER IN LITERATURE (ATL)

Developed by The Contemporary Arts Educational Project, Inc., a nonprofit corporation, and published through its Sun & Moon Press, the American Theater in Literature program was established to promote American theater as a literary form and to educate readers about contemporary and modern theater. The program publishes work of major American playwrights as well as younger, developing dramatists in various publishing programs of the Press, including the Sun & Moon Classics (collections of plays of international significance), the Mark Taper Forum Plays, Soho Rep Plays, Undermain Theatre Plays, Primary Stages Plays, and as a regular imprint of Sun & Moon Press.

BOOKS IN THIS PROGRAM

Len Jenkin *Dark Ride and Other Plays* ($13.95)
(Sun & Moon Classics: 22)
Robert Auletta *The Persians* ($9.95)
(A Mark Taper Forum Play)
Matthew Maguire *The Tower* ($8.95)
Kier Peters *The Confirmation* ($6.95)
Len Jenkin *Careless Love* ($9.95)
(A Soho Rep Play / Sun & Moon Classics: 54)
Mac Wellman *Two Plays: A Murder of Crows* and
The Hyacinth Macaw ($11.95)
(A Primary Stages Play / Sun & Moon Classics: 62)
Jeffrey Jones *Love Trouble* ($10.95)
(An Undermain Theatre Play / Sun & Moon Classics: 84)
David Greenspan *Son of an Engineer* ($8.95)
Matthew Maguire *Phaedra* ($8.95)

OTHER BOOKS OF THEATER FROM SUN & MOON PRESS

Eleanor Antin *Eleanora Antinova Plays* ($12.95)
Mac Wellman, ed., *Theatre of Wonders: Six Contemporary American Plays* ($12.95)
(Plays by Len Jenkin, Jeffrey Jones, Des McAnuff, Elizabeth Wray, and Mac Wellman)
Mac Wellman *The Professional Frenchman* ($8.95)
(A Blue Corner Book)
Jens Bjørneboe *The Bird Lovers* ($9.95)
(Sun & Moon Classics: 43)
Mac Wellman *Bad Penny* ($5.95)
(A Blue Corner Book)
Douglas Messerli *Silence All Round Marked: An Historical Play in Hysteria Writ* ($5.95)
(A Blue Corner Book)
Jerome Lawrence *A Golden Circle* ($19.95)
Joe Ross *Guards of the Heart* ($9.95)
(A Blue Corner Book)

Order from Sun & Moon Press, 6026 Wilshire Boulevard, Los Angeles, California 90036; (213) 857-1115.